INTRODUCTION

Standard Grade Drama is a two-year course of study.

Each school plans its own course to suit the needs of pupils. A series of units which focus on specific skills, themes or relationships provides a structured sequence of drama activities.

The course is broken down into three assessable elements: **Creating**, **Presenting** and **Knowledge and Understanding**.

As well as a grade for each element, your overall grade will be shown on your certificate. This is worked out from the average assessable element grade, for example:

Creating   Grade 2
Presenting   Grade 3
Knowledge and Understanding   Grade 4

Overall grade 2 + 3 + 4 = 9 divided by 3 (because there are 3 assessable elements) = 3

Creating and Presenting are assessed in class. Your teacher marks your work in Creating and Presenting.

Knowledge and Understanding is assessed in a written examination at the end of your course. At present there is one exam paper for all levels – Foundation, General and Credit. In future there may be a change to separate papers for different levels. An external examiner marks your Knowledge and Understanding exam paper.

This book suggests ways of giving your best performance in all three areas. You can use it from the beginning of your course in S3 right through to the end of S4.

It will help you with practical work and evaluations as well as the written exam.

You can't 'do drama' on your own. The work you do in class, with your teacher and with others is what really matters. This book is for you to study:

- when there is something you don't understand

- when you're stuck for ideas

- when you need help with evaluations

- before the exam, to remind you of the main things you need to know.

The book is divided into three sections, with each section covering one of the three elements: Creating, Presenting and Knowledge and Understanding. But they are all linked: your Presenting Evaluations are a way of describing what you did and what you learned from practical work; what you write about in the Knowledge and Understanding exam is based on work done in Creating and Presenting.

It is important to know the **right words** for what you do in drama. So, there is also a **Glossary** at the end of the book with useful drama words and what they mean. If you come across a word in this book which you don't know, look it up in the Glossary. If you learn and use these in discussion and writing, you will put your ideas across clearly. Your teacher will tell you which words you should learn and may add some more.

The most important thing to remember is that Drama is a subject which lets **you** put **your ideas** into action. If you do this, you will enjoy your work and get the grades you deserve.

CREATING

This Creating section will help you to come up with ideas for drama, working with other people and getting the most out of discussion and role-play.

Working from a Stimulus

What is a stimulus?

A stimulus is a starting point for drama, anything which suggests ideas that can be developed. Drama is a way of showing feelings and ideas. Like art and music, it allows us to share how we look at the world with others. To begin to create a drama, you need ideas. These can come from anything and anywhere. Drama is all around us – if you can see that, you will notice lots of things in everyday life which could be a starting point for drama.

For example:

people chatting on the bus

a television advert

a song on the radio

an old gravestone

Each of these could be a stimulus.

Examples of stimuli

★ **A photograph**

Who are the people in the picture? Where are they? What is going on? What has happened just before this? What will happen next? Think of some ways of turning this into a drama. Is one person the leader? Could something go wrong? What different ways could there be to make this into a story?

★ An object

In one drama lesson, a carrier bag was handed in for someone in the class. Everyone wondered what was in it – lunch, PE kit, a bomb… ? It became the stimulus for some interesting work.

Here are some other things you could start with:

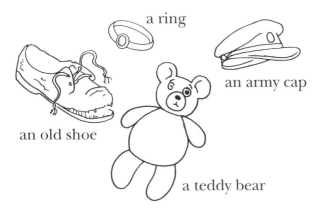

a ring

an army cap

an old shoe

a teddy bear

These could all have stories behind them and dramas created from them.

★ An old ballad
(a poem which tells a story)

Ballad of the Sea Horse

You landsmen and you seamen bold,
Attention give to me
While I a tragedy unfold
Upon the briny sea.

Who is telling this story? What was the tragedy, the terrible thing that happened at sea? This could give you ideas for a drama about a shipwreck or some other danger. Maybe the storyteller was the only one who lived to tell the tale.

★ A script

OLD MAN: Well, we'll be having another meal at 5.30. I thought we were just having a drink of tea now, but…

OLD LADY: There's no need to know…

OLD MAN: I don't, I'm not used to this sort of thing. What's that?

HELPER: Just chocolate.

OLD LADY: Just chocolate. I'll have a wee chocolate… No, thank you, that's quite enough – that's a record for me anyway. I love anything chocolatey.
Thank you.

OLD MAN: …have something like that in all the songs, you know. We think they're old songs, but that's what I remember about…

OLD LADY: Harrogate.

I used to come in my youth to Harrogate, to the Majestic and – what do you call the one that's closed now – the Grand…

HELPER: The Grand Hotel.

OLD LADY: …and dance there a lot. It was lovely.

This script has three characters. It could be used in several different ways. Think about who these old people are. What were their lives like when they were younger? Who are their families? What are their lives like now? You could show an adult son or daughter trying to decide about putting their parent into a home.

The old lady could be telling a grandchild about her own childhood. The old man might be remembering his war service; flashbacks (which show events from the past) could be used. Who is the helper? Why is she doing this work?

★ **Music**

 The music from *The X Files* could give you ideas, starting with a mood or atmosphere, then finding action to go with it.

The music suggests mystery; a build-up of tension; fast, repeated movements; figures seen for a moment in passing…

You could try this in movement only, with each person doing something suggested by the sounds. These movements might give you ideas for what could happen: a chase, a struggle.

This could lead on to a drama with speaking as well as action.

★ **A story or headline from a newspaper**

> **PRISONER WINS LEGAL ACCESS TO DAUGHTERS**
> Despite strong opposition from his ex-wife, a prisoner yesterday won access to the two children of his former marriage – which means they will be taken to see him in prison.

There are different ways of using this news story. The prison visit could be acted out.

You could find out the feelings of the different family members before or after it. One of the children might be trying to persuade her mother to let her see her father. The mother could be discussing the case with her lawyer.

You might wonder what the father did to be put in prison – this could be shown.

★ **Song lyrics**

can suggest feelings – lost love, happiness, regrets…

> I was once like you are now,
> And I know that it's not easy
> To be calm, when you've found
> Something going on.
>
> But take your time, think a lot,
> Why, think of everything you've got,
>
> For you will still be here tomorrow,
> But your dreams may not.

This could be a drama about how a father and son get on at a particular time in their lives – the father is middle-aged, the son a teenager.

It could look at a family over a number of years, showing how relationships change. There are lines in this song which could be spoken in the drama and added to.

★ **A proverb or saying**

is often something everyone knows. It can be fun to work with, creating a story which shows what it means.

For example:

> WHEN THE CAT'S AWAY THE
> MICE WILL PLAY.

One obvious idea would be for the 'cat', the parent in a family, to go away for the night, leaving the 'mice', the teenage son and daughter to 'play'. They have a party which could end up with the house being wrecked. This would work best as a drama if you showed how the people in it dealt with the problems.

Or you could show what happens when the 'cat', the boss, leaves the 'mice', the workers, in charge of an office or workshop. The workers have an important job to do. Things go wrong.

Here are two other proverbs you could use as starting points:

> EVERY CLOUD HAS A
> SILVER LINING.

> A STITCH IN TIME SAVES NINE.

★ **A sound effect**

Sounds of a forest at night or of a busy city street can make you feel you are in a real place. This can give you ideas for a drama.

The forest could be the place where you act out a fantastic story of magic and animals of the night.

The city street could show the lives of people there – rich, poor, busy, hungry, honest, criminal, lonely or part of a group.

★ **A plan**

could suggest a mystery, a secret meeting:

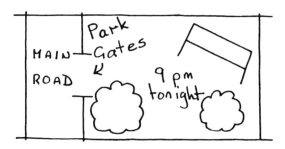

Who drew this? Why? Who would see this? Could someone find this by accident? What might happen?

You will be used to working from starting points like these in your classwork. For the exam, you will be given a range of stimuli to work from in the Stimulus Paper. Being open to lots of ideas and trying them out all through your course will help you work quickly and creatively.

Working in a Group

Sharing ideas with others

AND THE NEXT GROUP IS.....
LAURA   MARK   COLIN   KATE   AND   PAUL

OH GOOD, KATE HAS LOTS OF GOOD IDEAS. I CAN KEEP QUIET.

THAT PAUL MADE A FOOL OF ME IN MATHS.

MARK AND I CAN HAVE A LAUGH.

I'M GLAD I'M WITH LAURA. I DON'T KNOW ABOUT THE BOYS!

MARK CAN BE A PAIN, BUT I LIKE KATE.

When you are working from a stimulus, you will be sharing ideas and trying these out in a group with others.

> It is really important to be able to work with other people.

In the Drama class, you don't need to be in a group with your friends. Sometimes it is better to work with someone you don't know so well. Your teacher needs to see you working with **different** people. Everyone should be able to work with everyone else.

Sometimes there is someone that no-one wants to work with. What if it's you? No-one likes to feel left out or not wanted. In Drama everyone has something to give to the group. But some people need extra help. To say 'We're not working with her,' is hurtful and often unfair. Drama can help people get on with others, if they're given a chance.

Of course, if someone is behaving badly – shouting, refusing to listen, upsetting other people – you can't get on. That's when you'll need help from your teacher. But as you get better at working with others, your drama work will improve.

Often you have to work to a **deadline** (a time by which the task must be finished), so it is important not to waste time. Here are some skills you can practise to make sure you and your group do good work in a short time:

★ **Find a space to work in**

Make sure that everyone in the group can be seen and heard. Try not to be too close to another group – you don't want to be put off by hearing what they are saying. Start by making sure that everyone is clear about what to do. Have you all read or looked at the stimulus material? What has the teacher asked you to do? How long do you have to work on this? Setting yourselves a **time limit** for talking is useful. Sometimes it helps if someone notes down ideas, perhaps on a large sheet of paper with a marker pen. Then you have a record of what is said. You might each want to use this later to write your own notes.

★ **Offer ideas**

Everyone's ideas are useful and important, so feel you can suggest something even if it doesn't seem very exciting or original. When lots of ideas are suggested and listened to or noted down, this is called **brainstorming**. This can be a good way to begin.

★ **Listen to others**

Encourage quieter people to speak – help them by agreeing: 'That's worth thinking about,' and by asking questions: 'What would she do then?'

★ **Say what you think**

without being critical: 'That's a really good idea, but I think we need to make it simpler.'

★ **Develop ideas**

Build on what other people have said, adding your suggestions:

'We could have the old sailor telling the story…'

'Yes, he could sit at one side…'

'Then, if there was a flashback to show the shipwreck…'

'Maybe we could do that just with movement and with the sounds of the storm?'

★ **Try out ideas**

Get the group up on their feet and **improvise**, acting out the ideas you have been talking about, without planning, to find out what happens. Sort out a working space, re-arranging chairs, checking that you are not disturbing other groups.

Now you have ideas which you like, you need to think about how to act them out. This will mean people **adopting roles**, taking them on for a short time to see what happens when you put your ideas into action.

★ **Select and reject ideas**

Choose ideas and decide which ones work. Go on with those ideas and forget about the ones which don't work. Be honest with each other about this:

'We could just have the older girl visiting the dad in prison, then we would find out more about how she gets on with him.'

'Showing the robbery is going to be difficult – maybe we could have a TV news report about it.'

'No, we can't possibly act out the whole of the trial. Why don't we just show him being sentenced?'

If something isn't working, sit down for a few minutes and talk it through. Sometimes looking at it from a **different angle** can be helpful. If you feel it would be hard to show a boy being hit by his angry father, you could have the boy telling his friend about what happened, or the father trying to explain it to his wife afterwards.

Always keep in mind that your ideas have to be practical, workable from a drama point of view. Ten helicopters landing, or a tidal wave, could be very difficult to show in your drama space!

★ **Solve problems**

as you go along. Try to consider each other and to solve arguments by giving choices.

Remember that drama can bring out **real feelings.** Maybe you know that someone could be upset by working on an idea about divorce or bullying. Make sure that you deal with this before final decisions are made.

If you are usually seen as the one with all the ideas, sit back and listen for a while, encouraging others.

If you find it hard to put your ideas across, try adding to what someone else has said, agreeing or suggesting something different, building up your confidence gradually.

★ **Make notes**

Allow yourselves time for this and write down what ideas were tried out, what worked and which material could be developed. Discuss any research which needs to be done. **Research** is finding out information which will help make your Drama believable. For example, if you were showing a prison visit or a court scene you could try to find out what happens in real life. Decide who will do this. Write down reasons for choices and decisions made. Some of this might be done as homework and used in the next practical lesson.

Everything you write down is useful for later on.

Using role-play to try out ideas

Role-play is a way of finding out what people might say or do in an **imaginary** situation. In role you behave **as if** you are, for example, in charge, nervous, friendly or being bullied.

★ **Improvise right away without too much planning**

Agree quickly on who will play which role – it doesn't matter at this stage who does what – it's simply a question of seeing if an idea works.

Imagine your group is working from the stimulus which is this plan:

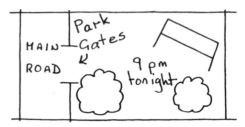

You decide to act out the meeting between two members of a gang. First, you need a suitable space to suggest the **location** (the place where the drama happens). Two chairs are placed side by side to be a bench in a park. One person sits on the bench, waiting. A second member of the gang comes in from one side, running. They begin to talk. This is where others in the group watch those who are taking part and suggest ideas:

'The guy who ran in seems scared. What's he frightened of?'

This can lead you on to another scene, perhaps just before the meeting, where you see what has happened to this person. Maybe a **prop** (an object to use in the drama) is needed:

'Let's give her a bag; it's got something in it that he wants.'

'He's not nearly frightening enough; he should be shouting at her.'

This is a time to **try things out**, not to criticise the way someone acts out ideas.

You could ask someone who has a suggestion to take over a role:

'Paul, you do the bad guy this time; show us how you think it should be done.'

But, remember, you are just being asked to adopt a role – to show you feel frightened or angry – not to develop a character in any depth. **There is no need to practise scenes at this point.** Decide if the idea works: if it does, note it for working on later; if not, try something else.

Using space and other resources

Space is wherever you are working. It's useful to decide where your acting area begins and ends.

Resources are anything available which you can make use of in your work.

★ **Talk about what you might need**

Don't start making detailed plans about how to use scenery or costumes at the moment. Experiment with any resources which are handy, for example:

- rostra (blocks or platforms)
- percussion instruments (drums, tambourines, bells)
- masks
- pieces of cloth

Make imaginary use of **space** and **objects**:

'This area is the path – we could have a tree here for him to hide behind…'

'Then she takes out her mobile phone…'

'He suddenly sees the knife on the ground…'

Be ready to try ideas out in **different ways**. Here are some you could try:

- dialogue (speaking) and action
- movement
- tableaux (still or frozen pictures)
- interviews
- narration (where someone tells the story)
- flashbacks (showing earlier events)
- mime

Remember that a scene which doesn't work as dialogue and action might work really well in mime.

Try not to get carried away – one group acting out a noisy argument at full volume can make it hard for others to concentrate.

How is your work in Creating marked?

Your teacher will watch and listen to you as you are working and may use a checklist to note down what he or she sees you doing. Over your two-year course, he or she will build up a record of your abilities and progress in Creating.

This record will be used towards the end of the course to help the teacher decide on your final Creating grade. It is likely that you will make steady progress over two years, building up your skills as you gain experience.

By the end of the Creating process, your teacher should have seen you giving ideas, taking on different roles and making use of space and other resources (real or imaginary).
You and your group now have some ideas which you can develop for presenting to an audience.

PRESENTING

In this Presenting section you will find ideas to help you prepare your drama to show to an audience. This section also includes advice on how to do your evaluations.

How are you going to present your Drama?

Having studied the Creating Section, you are now ready to move onto the next stage – preparing your work for presenting to an audience. From the Creating work you have done you have some ideas based on role-play and improvised drama, along with research – which can be developed into a presentation.

Content, Form and Structure

★ **Content**

You must first decide what your drama is about. This is called its **content**.

Then you must work out how to perform it so that an audience will understand it. This means deciding on the right **form** and **structure**.

★ **Form**

means **how** the drama is presented, for example:

- Mime
- Dance drama
- Monologue (where one person speaks alone)
- Puppet show
- Rehearsed improvisation

★ **Structure**

is the way in which time, place and action are put together, for example:

- Scene 1 – morning, kitchen
- Scene 2 – afternoon, the park
- Scene 3 – evening, kitchen

A scene is a part of a drama which happens in one place and at one time.

Writing a scenario

It's useful to begin with a scenario (an **outline** of the drama) in which the storyline is worked out. This should include details of the time and place of the action.

Imagine you have been working from the script of the two old people talking (on page 5). Your group, through discussion and role-play, has decided to develop this into a drama in which a family has to decide if they should put an elderly relative into a nursing home. You will need to show the audience how the family relate to one another and the situation they are in.

This could be done by improvising realistic scenes showing family life. You may also want the audience to understand and sympathise with the old person. This could be done by using monologues in which this character speaks his thoughts, or by including flashbacks which show scenes from his younger life. These are likely to be ideas you have already tried out in Creating.

Here are some notes for a possible scenario:

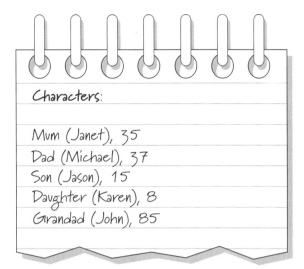

Characters:

Mum (Janet), 35
Dad (Michael), 37
Son (Jason), 15
Daughter (Karen), 8
Grandad (John), 85

Scenario:

Monday morning, kitchen. Mum, Dad, teenage son having breakfast. Daughter, getting ready for school, complains that Grandad is in the bathroom. Triggers discussion about difficulties of having him to stay.

Later that day, kitchen. Grandad sitting at table. Daughter comes in from school, upset. They start talking.

Flashback to Grandad at school, being bullied.

Back to present time. Grandad gives Daughter advice.

This could be continued, with more realistic scenes showing present day life, with flashbacks showing that the Grandad has knowledge and experience which can help the family. But the problems,

arguments and hurt feelings could also be shown. At the end of the drama the Grandad might decide to leave his family and go into a home.

- Deciding how you are going to present your drama is very important because this is when you have to select and reject material.

- You need to be realistic about what you can do in the time you have available.

- Don't make the mistake of trying to act out too many scenes using different locations. Even one scene change in a ten-minute presentation can get in the way of the drama.

- Try to have a definite beginning, middle and end.

- Give each person in the group one main part to play.

- Be clear about what you want the audience to understand.

You can find out more about **Content, Form** and **Structure** on pages 24 – 31.

Building your Character

In role-play you have been developing an imaginary situation as yourself or another person, looking at how someone might react or behave. Now that you have a character to develop, you have the chance to create an individual personality within a drama, to portray a specific, definite role in depth.

You will do this as you play your part in different scenes, but there is a lot of work you can do yourself to make your character believable.

Here is how you might build the character of the Grandad in the drama we have been thinking about:

★ **How old is he?**

Eighty-five, old enough to have served in the Second World War.

★ **What has happened in his life?**

He grew up on a farm with his parents and his younger sister, Mary. He left school at 14 and became an apprentice baker. In 1939 he joined the army. He served in Burma, where he was a prisoner of war for two years. After the war, he married his wife Jean and they had a daughter, Janet. He retired from the bakery and led an active life until he had a stroke six months ago. His wife died last year.

★ **What is he called?**

The children call him Grandad, but his name is John Macdonald.

★ **What does he look like?**

Grey hair, parted at one side, wrinkles on forehead and around eyes, reddish cheeks and nose, grey moustache.

★ **What does he wear?**

Glasses, a checked shirt and tie, a woollen cardigan, corduroy trousers with a belt, slippers.

★ **What is he like as a person?**

He is basically good-natured and kind, but has been upset by his wife's death and his own illness. He tends to get annoyed by little things these days.

★ **How does he speak?**

Loudly and fast to tell Jason to turn down his music; quietly and sadly to Janet about his wife's death; kindly to Karen about school.

★ **How does he move?**

Slowly and stiffly because of his rheumatic knees; clumsily at times if he feels dizzy.

★ **What does he like to do?**

He used to enjoy fishing and going to the pub with his friends, but hasn't managed to get out much recently.

★ **Why does he do that?**

Asking questions like 'Why do you do that?' can help you understand how to play the part. You can do this by 'hot-seating' the character, who then answers in role. Here are some questions your group could ask the person playing Grandad:

'Why do you get so angry when Jason doesn't answer?'

'Why don't you ever offer to help get meals ready?'

'How did you feel when Karen came home crying?'

'What is your worst fear?'

★ **How does he get on with other people?**

He loves his family, but sometimes he finds Michael hard to speak to. He doesn't like Jason's friends. He thinks they are rude and noisy.

★ **How important is he compared with other people in the drama?**

Do others look up to him? Why? He may feel much less important now than when he was fit and well. But he is important to others in different ways. His position may change as the drama goes on.

★ **How does he feel and think?**

Writing in role is a way of getting into the mind of your character.

This could be a letter written by John to another relative:

> Dear Mary,
>
> I have been staying with Janet and her family since I came out of hospital. They have been very kind, but I feel they don't really want me here. Michael is busy with his work and I feel I get in Janet's way. Wee Karen is just lovely and likes to hear my stories about the old days, but all Jason seems to want to do is listen to this terrible noise he calls music. He has no respect for his parents. I don't know what to do. I can't go back to my own house because of these dizzy turns I keep taking. I suppose it'll need to be a nursing home, but I can't say I like the idea very much. Try to come and see me soon.
>
> Your loving brother,
> John

★ **How can you make him more believable?**

Watching and listening to some real elderly men to see how they move and speak could give you some ideas. Look at things they do, like head-shaking, ear-pulling, coughing, fiddling with glasses. Listen to how they speak, the words they use:

'Let me tell you, son…'

'The things you see…'

'We never used to…'

Working on your character in this way will help you work out how to behave in the drama. If your character is **convincing**, the audience will believe in you.

You can find more about **Building a Character** on pages 31 – 36.

What about your Audience?

Where will your audience sit?

- In rows in front of the performing area?

- On three sides?

- How close do you want them to be to the actors?

What you decide depends on what you want them to see.

For the Grandad drama, you might want your audience on three sides. That way they can be involved with what the family are feeling. They will be able to see the expressions on the performers' faces if they sit fairly close to the acting area.

You can find more about **Staging your Presentation** on pages 36 and 37.

Who are your audience?

- Your own class?

- Primary school children?

- Adults?

- Is your drama suitable for your audience?

The Grandad drama could be understood by younger children. One of the characters is primary school age, and most children know about grandparents.

But if you wanted to show a serious argument, maybe with some violence, it might be better to have an older audience.

If you want to help different generations understand each other, you might want all age groups to see it.

KU You can find more about **Target Audience** on page 38.

★ **What do you want your audience to think about?**

You would want them to think about what it feels like to be old, to feel that you are not wanted. You might want teenagers to be a bit more considerate towards their grandparents; you might want grandparents to understand teenagers better.

★ **How do you want your audience to feel?**

You might want them to feel sorry for Grandad and for Janet, his daughter, for having to put up with him. You might want them to feel worried about Karen being bullied at school, or about what Jason is doing with his friends.

KU You can find more about **Meaning and Message** on pages 38 – 40.

Drawing a ground plan

Before you start rehearsing (practising and improving your drama) you need to agree on **how to use the space** for presenting your drama. Draw a plan to show the stage area, where the audience will be, where performers come in and go out (the exits and entrances) and where any furniture or rostra will be placed. Put in any important props.

Your plan should be a **bird's eye view** of the acting area, drawn roughly to scale and with a key to show what symbols you have used. This will help you set up quickly for each rehearsal.

Here is a ground plan for the first scene of the Grandad drama, in the kitchen:

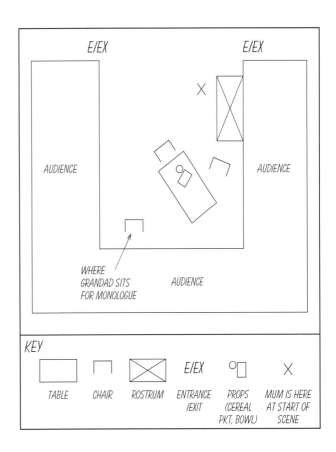

Adding Theatre Arts

Theatre Arts include **make-up**, **costume**, **sound**, **music**, **lighting**, **scenery**, **furniture** and **props**. They can make your drama better, more interesting and believable. Using them can be very creative and enjoyable and gives you the chance to practise your skills in theatre technology.

Theatre technology is the equipment you need to create effects, for example a tape recorder and a lighting control desk. Technical work is any work done using Theatre Arts and technology.

Time is often short and resources have to be shared among groups – this can be frustrating. So, you have to plan and negotiate with others and your teacher. This means talking about difficulties and sorting them out fairly.

Start by discussing as a group **what you need to do** and **how you can get it done**. Is some research needed – into historical costumes, for example? **Be realistic** about what you can do in the time you have and with the resources available.

★ **Make-up and costume**  can help you **develop** a **character**.

Here are some ideas that could be used in the Grandad drama:

- *Grandad*
  Old age base, a touch of red cream make-up on cheeks and nose, dark shading and highlight for wrinkles on forehead and under eyes. White powder on hair, grey crêpe hair moustache.

- *Karen*
  Primary school sweatshirt, short skirt, hair in bunches, white knee socks.

★ **Sound, music and lighting**

 add **mood** and **atmosphere**. Here are some ideas that could be used in the Grandad drama:

- sounds of gunfire and explosions for a flashback showing Grandad's army service in the Second World War

- loud, techno music off stage (Jason's room)

- a spotlight on Grandad for a monologue where he talks about leaving the family.

★ **Scenery, furniture and props**

provide a **realistic** or **fantastic** setting.

Here are some ideas:

- black cloth draped over a screen to suggest the hut where Grandad is kept prisoner in a wartime flashback

- a table and two chairs for the kitchen

- a doll for Karen to play with

- a letter which arrives from Great Aunt Mary.

★ **Decide who is going to be in charge of each task**

Make sure they know what to do and where to get help.

Plan ahead – someone may be absent at a critical point. Have someone else lined up to help out.

PAUL'S OFF. WHAT ARE WE GOING TO DO?

THERE'S NO POINT IN TRYING TO DO ANY WORK TODAY!

IT'S OK, THE LIGHTING CUES ARE IN THE FOLDER.

WE CAN DO THE SCENES THAT THE DAD'S NOT IN.

★ **Troubleshooting**

Usually, several groups will be trying to do technical work at the same time. This can cause problems. You must sort out **who** does **what**, and **when**.

Be prepared to be **flexible** – get on with rehearsing while another group position their lights. Maybe someone could make a sound tape at home and save time in class. Try to make sure **everyone** in the group has a job to do – if two of you have a scene to rehearse, other group members could be doing make-up designs or writing up props lists.

Often, ideas are too complicated and ambitious for the time and resources available. Sometimes a really good idea will have to be changed because it just can't be done. Even if you can't use it, you can write later about what you **would** have done. Ideas are never wasted – they

can be used another time. Stop now and then to review progress, discussing and noting down problems. Being able to adapt and **simplify** can help your group meet deadlines.

Last minute technical problems **always** happen: be ready for this. Have scissors, tape, safety pins, torch, copies of plans and lists handy. A spare tape recorder or alternative spotlight can allow the show to go on.

For all technical work, keeping careful notes, plans and lists is absolutely essential. **Keep everything safely in a folder in school** and make sure everyone in the group knows where it is.

Sometimes you will want someone to be your **stage manager**, to be responsible for everything on the technical side while the rest of you are acting. This can be a very rewarding and challenging job. Doing this at some point in your Standard Grade course will help you understand more about using Theatre Arts.

KU You can find more about **Theatre Arts** on pages 40 – 44.

The Performance

The audience is waiting.

Your mouth goes dry and you've forgotten everything.

You take a few deep breaths and relax your shoulders.

The lights go up, and you're on!

Amazingly, you get through it, remembering what you did in rehearsals.

You even add something new and it works.

Someone makes a mistake but the rest of you help them out.

The audience doesn't notice.

You get to the end, much faster than you expected.

The audience claps.

They liked it!

You've done it!

And it feels great... But now you're going to have to evaluate it.

Evaluations

Talking and writing about what you have done yourself

Evaluating your own work is the final stage of the Presenting process. Evaluating means looking back at what you've done, reflecting on how effective it was and asking yourself if you achieved what you set out to do. But you don't have to do it all by yourself. You and your group can give each other a lot of help and support at this stage too. Keeping notes, lists and plans as you go along will make it easier to write (or tape) a detailed account of what you did and what you learned. Your teacher will give you guidance on how to do this, but here are some things which you could usefully think about. Remember to **justify** (give reasons for) everything you say.

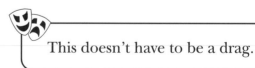

This doesn't have to be a drag.

The last thing you want to do is to kill that good feeling you got when you did your presentation.

★ **Before writing (or taping) your evaluation of your own presentation:**

- Write down some words that your presentation made you think of:

  magic, sad, feelings, understanding, conflict, problems, trust, atmosphere, laughter, tension.

- Sit down and talk with someone from your group. Talk about the best bits, the worst bits and what you felt pleased about.

- Do the same with someone from another group. Ask what they thought of your presentation. Tell them what you thought of theirs.

- You may be able to watch a video recording of your presentation which you can discuss with your class.

- Talk with your teacher about your contribution.

★ **Include these points in your evaluation of your own presentation:**

- Your evaluation is of Presenting, not of Creating, so begin at the point where you started to prepare your drama to present to your audience.

- Say what you were asked to do and how you decided on what material to develop for your presentation. Be clear about your personal contribution right from the start.

- Mention ideas that you put forward, even if they were rejected. Write about how the group worked out a storyline, how you decided who should play which part. Were there disagreements? Say what the problems were and how you solved them. Give reasons for your decisions.

- Include what ideas you had about the character you were to play. Did you have any other tasks, for example, finding music or making props?

- Say how rehearsals went. Were there particular problems – use of space, entrances and exits, developing characters – that had to be sorted out?

- Describe how you went about developing your own character. Mention language and voice, movement, working on relationships through improvised drama and discussion. Did your character change?

- Say what use your group made of Theatre Arts. Give reasons for what you chose to use, any problems you came across and how these were solved.

- State what your group's aim was in the presentation. What did you want your audience to think and feel?

- Say what made it work. What did you learn?

- Remember to justify everything you say.

Talking and writing about what you have seen other people do

When you've seen a really good presentation, either in the classroom or in a theatre, you're left with a feeling of 'Wow! That was amazing!'

That's what you want to build on when you do an evaluation of others.

What made it special?

What was there that gave you that feeling – the 'tingle factor' – that has you sitting straight up in your seat?

Was it the actor who made you laugh till you cried?

Was it the set, where the revolving stage swung round to show the soldiers ready for battle?

Was it the eerie bell tolling on a darkened stage?

Work on this in the same way as your evaluation of your own presentation. Use your own knowledge and experience to help you judge others.

★ **Before writing (or taping) your evaluation of others:**

  · Write down some words that the presentation made you think of:

    powerful, exciting, laughter, effects, music, fighting, wonder, real, movement, colour, mood, startling.

  · Sit down and talk with someone else who saw it. Talk about the best bits, the worst bits, and what you remember most clearly.

  · Look at the programme. There is lots of useful information in this about the play, the actors, the director, the designer and others.

  · Talk with your teacher. He or she may have some ideas of his or her own, or some questions for you.

★ **Include these points in your evaluations of other presentations:**

  · Say where you saw it. Did you see the presentation in a big theatre or a school hall? Were you close to the actors? What made you feel involved?

  · Say what happened in the presentation.

  · Who was it aimed at? (Target Audience?)

  · Include the best moments. Why were they the best?

  · Describe a couple of good acting performances in some detail (use your programme for names). You know enough about building a character to be critical.

  · Discuss Theatre Arts. How did make-up, costume, sound, music, lighting, scenery, furniture and props help make the presentation special?

  · Say what made it work. How did it make you feel? What did it make you think about?

  · What was your overall opinion?

  · Remember to justify everything you say.

How is your work in Presenting marked?

For your practical work, your teacher will watch you and listen to you as you are working and may use a checklist to note down what he or she sees you doing. Over your two-year course, he or she will build up a record of your skills and progress in Presenting.

He or she will also be marking the evaluations you will be doing, which could be written or taped. Towards the end of the course, your two best evaluations, one of self and one of others, will be chosen. Your teacher will give you a grade for these. This grade will be combined with your final grade for your practical work to give an overall grade for Presenting.

By the end of the Presenting process, your teacher should have seen you helping to plan a Presentation, portraying a character and showing you can use Theatre Arts. You will also have shown that you can evaluate your own drama work and the work of others.

You can now go on to the Knowledge and Understanding Section to study Drama in more detail to prepare for your exam.

KNOWLEDGE AND UNDERSTANDING

In this Knowledge and Understanding section you will find more detailed information about topics mentioned in the Presenting section, including advice on working from a script. In this section there is also help with preparing for and sitting the exam.

Content, Form and Structure

 Check back to page 12 for an introduction to Content, Form and Structure.

Deciding on Content

When you begin to think about presenting your work, you start with something you want to communicate to an audience. Through discussion and experimenting with ideas, you come up with a story, a feeling or a message you want to share with others. You select material which has **dramatic potential**. This material is the content of your drama. Within this material you must have a **focus** for your drama – the main aspects of it that you want the audience to concentrate on.

Having decided **what** you want to communicate in your drama (its content), you now have to decide **how** to do this (its form and structure).

Choosing the right Form

Form is the **overall style** of your presentation, for example: rehearsed improvisation, scripted presentation, movement, dance drama, mime, documentary, radio play, puppet show, musical, soap opera, chat show, monologue.

You can use the **same** form throughout your drama or show ideas using different **conventions**. These are alternative ways of presenting **all** or **part(s)** of your work, for example: tableau, soliloquy, flashback, voice over, narration, slow motion. Here are some forms and conventions you could use:

★ **Movement**

Creative movement can be a powerful way of **expressing emotion**. You may want to present your drama purely as a movement piece, or have only one scene using this convention. Once you have your initial idea, there are different ways of developing it. You may already have a piece of music – this will suggest movements which can be improvised to it. If you are starting with movements, you might want to find suitable sound effects or music to go with them.

Try out different positioning and groupings – individual, pairs, threes… Make contact in different ways. Experiment with levels, rhythm, speed and balance. Take turns to watch – what shapes are emerging, what feelings are coming across? Remember that stillness can be effective – try freezing a movement, or one figure.

Look at making interesting use of space. Improvised movement can be a good way of communicating a mood or a feeling.

★ Dance drama

To take a creative movement piece further, you would rehearse and develop it, making it more **stylised**, perhaps using movement to tell a story. Your teacher might direct it, or you might work in groups, giving the improvised sequence a clearer shape. This could then be described as a dance drama.

It doesn't mean that you have to be a dancer! You may have someone in your group who has a **special interest** in dance – contemporary, jazz, Highland, ballet or tap. Maybe they could teach the group some steps and movements which could be adapted for your piece, but this is not essential.

Rehearsals need planning – your group will probably need extra space and the chance to rehearse with music. Warming up and winding down at the beginning and end of each rehearsal are important; maybe you could each take a turn to lead these.

★ Mime

is another **stylised** form of movement, which creates an illusion of reality, using exaggerated movement, body language, gestures and facial expression to communicate with the audience.

Mime can be very suitable for some material – for example, a comic sequence or a serious funeral ceremony. It needs planning and rehearsal; **exact timing** of actions is important.

★ Documentary

involves making use of **factual material** – newspaper articles, historical documents or biographies – to present a dramatic investigation. This is a way of exploring a theme or issue, such as Poverty or War, or of telling the story of a real event, such as The Tay Bridge Disaster. This type of drama is often used to put across a **message**. You would start by doing research, collecting information and improvising scenes. Your aim would be to make a presentation which would help an audience understand more about your chosen topic.

★ Radio play

Having a sound recording as your end product can be an interesting way to present your ideas. Having to communicate everything through **voice** and **sound effects** is challenging – it can be a good way of practising voice and technical skills.

You can produce a radio play with just an ordinary cassette recorder and a microphone; a second cassette player and recordings of some sound effects will give you more scope. If you have the use of a mixing desk, which allows you to record different tracks, you can be more ambitious.

Careful planning, practice with the equipment and plenty of time for rehearsing and recording are essential.

★ **Masks**

can provide a completely different kind of drama. You may have **plain white** masks to use, or **character** masks with particular expressions; you could even make your own.

As soon as you put on a mask which hides your facial expression, you become free to experiment with gestures and movement to express feelings. You can improvise on your own – working in front of a mirror can be helpful. Trying out ideas with others, allowing the masked characters to interact, can produce exciting results.

It does take time to develop mask work, so you must be realistic about rehearsal time.

★ **Puppets**

can be a useful way of giving a drama a different slant. You may have these already or be able to make them fairly quickly if time and resources allow. We tend to think of **glove** puppets or **string** puppets used to entertain young audiences, but there are other types which can be used in all kinds of presentations: **shadow** puppets can be dramatic and menacing; **life-size stick** puppets held by actors can become dancing partners or part of a crowd.

Puppets are not just for children's shows, but can be used in a serious drama. Imagine a teenager trying to make a major decision – should she stay on at school to sit her exams or leave to take up an offer of work as a model? You could have two simple puppets (glove or stick?) – one an angel, one a devil.

They could argue the two sides of the issue in an entertaining way which would help the audience understand the teenager's conflicting feelings.

★ **Multimedia**

Using technology – video, computer generated images, slides, and overhead projections – can provide either a **background to action** or a **separate focus** for the audience. A drama on homelessness could include projected photographs of life on the streets, lists of statistics or the silhouette of a city skyline to help communicate ideas.

Experimenting with Structure

The structure of your presentation will help the audience understand it, leading up to **key moments** and to the **central point** in the drama. You can choose a **linear** structure where the action unfolds from beginning to middle to end, or a **non-linear** structure where the action unfolds through shifts in time and place. Having decided on a **focus**, you would then structure the drama to make this focus clear to the audience, using suitable conventions.

You could start with a feeling which you want to explore. Drawing a web (also called a concept map) can give you ideas to use in your presentation. This one is about fear:

Here is a linear (chronological) scenario which could be developed from this:

A teenager is walking home at night along a lighted street with two friends. They reach the park gates. He says goodbye to his friends and sets out to take a short cut through the park. He starts to feel frightened, looking around nervously, jumping at any sounds. He starts whistling to himself and walks faster as he hears footsteps behind him. A woman walking her dog catches up, says 'Good evening,' and walks on. He hears footsteps again. This time, two men come up behind him. One grabs hold of him, the other threatens him, asking for money. They take his wallet and kick him to the ground. He lies there, hurt and frightened. The dog walker comes back, finds him and helps him to his feet.

Here is a non-linear structure using some of the same ideas:

A girl lies curled up in the centre of the performing space. She has a pillow, a blanket and a doll.

There is eerie music and four masked figures creep in at floor level. They take away her protective symbols — the pillow, doll and blanket — tossing them to one another, then off to the side. She is awake now and they pull her to her feet, then push her back and forward,

chanting in turn; 'You're ugly', 'You're a failure', 'Nobody likes you', 'You're stupid'. She sinks down, covering her ears, making herself as small as possible as the voices get louder and the figures more menacing. The figures now have a large piece of red cloth which they hold at each corner. They make it billow up above her, then let it fall to cover her. She screams. The figures shrink to the floor and creep away, pulling the cloth with them. Two of them return her props and she lies down peacefully.

> Remember, the stimulus is simply a **starting point**. You can take it **anywhere** you like. Your end product can be quite different from your initial ideas. That's what's so great about being allowed to be creative!

How to work from a script

Most of the work you do in drama is improvised, where you make up the words you say. But in the theatre, most plays you see are **written down** as a script. The script is what the actors and the director have to work from. If you have read some plays aloud, you will know that it is quite hard to bring the characters to life in the way that you are used to doing in your own improvised dramas.

If you are keen to try something challenging, working from a script can be very rewarding. If you go on with drama beyond Standard Grade, you will be doing more work using scripts. Here are some things to think about:

✓ Some good points about using a script	Some bad points about using a script ✗
The storyline is worked out for you.	You have to stick to the storyline.
You don't have to think what to say.	You have to learn lines.
You get some ideas about moves.	You have to work out moves.

It takes quite a lot of time to take a script from page to stage, so it makes sense to work on a short piece to start with.

★ **Working from page to stage**

- **Each person** in the group should have **a copy** of the script which can be written on, in pencil. A pencil with a rubber on the end is a good idea – you can easily make changes with it.

- Give each person **a part** to read; it doesn't matter who reads which part just now. It's useful if one person can read the stage directions, so you can picture what's going on.

- Talk about what happens and what you think the characters are like. Work out where and when the drama is happening. Do some **improvised** drama, **adopting roles** from the script, to help understand it better.

- Now **cast it**; by now you should have an idea about who should play which part. It's a good idea if one of you can watch, listen and suggest ideas, taking on responsibility to direct. The director has to work out what the writer of the script is trying to put across to an audience. If you are

directing, you need to have ideas about what the meaning and message is. **Read it** through **again**, with each of you now reading your own character's lines.

- Now you are ready to begin **blocking** your scene. Blocking means deciding where and when characters will move on stage and marking moves on the script.

★ **Using Stage Directions**

It helps when you're working on any drama (scripted or improvised) to be able to **communicate quickly** and **easily** with each other. Using words which are recognised in the theatre is a good idea. They seem confusing at first. This is because they go back to the old type of theatre where the stage was raked, sloping up from the audience so that the actors could be seen.

Here's a quick reference guide, with abbreviations (which save writing time):

Stage Direction	Abbreviation	Meaning
stage left	SL	actor's left
stage right	SR	actor's right
centre stage	CS	in the middle of the stage
up stage	US	area furthest from audience
down stage	DS	area nearest audience
move	→	go anywhere on stage
cross	✕	move from one side of stage to the other
turn	↙	move round
enter	E	come in
exit	Ex	go out
on stage	On	in the scene being played
off stage	Off	area close to the stage

Simple Stage Plan

USR	USC	USL	USR – Up Stage Right USC – Up Stage Centre USL – Up Stage Left
CSR	CS	CSL	CSR – Centre Stage Right CS – Centre Stage CSL – Centre Stage Left
DSR	DSC	DSL	DSR – Down Stage Right DSC – Down Stage Centre DSL – Down Stage Left

Audience

Decide on staging. Where will the audience be? Where are your entrances and exits? You need to do a rough ground plan and to find some rehearsal furniture, just as you would for an improvised drama. Get the group on their feet, with scripts and pencils in their hands. Now each person says their lines, but works out where they will stand, when they will move and what they will do. This needs good **teamwork**.

 Listening to everyone's ideas is really important.

The **director** is responsible for making the scene work, to help bring the script to life, but it is still a group effort. Write down your moves as you go along.

Here is what a few lines from one actor's (the Helper's) script might look like:

```
OLD LADY:  Harrogate.  I used to
come in my youth to Harrogate,
to the Majestic and - what do
you call the one that's closed
now - the Grand...
turn to OL take her r. hand in l.
hand (chocs in r. hand) looking at her smiling

HELPER: The Grand Hotel.
         (warmly) holding her hand

OLD LADY:  ...and dance there a
lot.  It was lovely.
     lay OL's hand in lap move off R
```

One script can be used as the **prompt copy**, on which all the moves are written down. This is the record of everything decided in rehearsals and is used to make sure everyone knows what they have to do in the performance.

Blocking is the slowest and often hardest bit. Be patient, stay calm.

Now you can get down to **serious rehearsing**. Without the script in your hand you can really get into character. This is when you will feel the drama coming to life.

You might feel that you spend a lot of time hanging about, waiting to be involved, but you can learn a lot from watching. If you're waiting to go on or are already on stage without any lines, it's important to **follow the script closely**. Make sure you don't miss your **cue** (the word or signal for you to speak or move).

While rehearsals are going on, anyone in the group not needed for a scene can be getting on with **technical work**. As with any presentation, you will need to organise make-up, costumes, sound, lighting, scenery, furniture and props. Designs, lists, plans, lighting and sound plots need to be prepared.

Once you have decided where and when lighting and sound effects are needed, cues for these can be added to the prompt copy. It might look something like this: (see next page)

LIGHTING	SOUND
LX 1 Bright indoor lighting.	SFX 1 Background sounds of people chatting, cups and saucers clattering. Fade down as OM speaks. Keep at low level all through scene.
	SFX 2 Piano begins to play 'As Time Goes By'. This continues quietly all through rest of scene.
LX 2 Fade general state. Bring up spot on OL.	

OM [[OM] OL [OL] H
R ⌐ ⌐ L

1 OM looks at watch.
2 shakes his head

3 H moves downstage to stand L. of OL with box.
4 OM notices box of chocolates.

5 OL chooses a chocolate.
6 H offers box again.

7 OL puts chocolate in mouth.
8 H moves centre stage, offers box to OM but he doesn't notice.
9 OM hums along with the piano music.

10 OL turns to H, holding up right hand.

11 H turns back to OL, takes her hand.

12 H lays OL's hand in her lap and moves off R

LX 1
SFX 1

OLD MAN: 1 Well, we'll be having another meal at 5.30. 2 I thought we were just having a drink of tea now, but... (confused)

OLD LADY: There's no need to know...
3

OLD MAN: I don't, I'm not used to this sort of thing. 4 What's that? (sharply)

HELPER: Just chocolate. (brightly)

OLD LADY: Just chocolate. 5 I'll have a wee chocolate... 6 No, (shakes head) thank you, that's quite enough – that's a record for me anyway. I love anything chocolatey. Thank you. 7
SFX 2

8
OLD MAN: 9 ...have something like that in all the songs, you know. We think they're old songs, but that's what I remember about...
LX 2

OLD LADY: Harrogate. I used to come in my youth to Harrogate, to the Majestic 10 and - what do you call the one that's closed now – the Grand...

HELPER: 11 The Grand Hotel.

OLD LADY: ...and dance there a lot. It 12 was lovely. (closes her eyes and smiles, remembering)

If you are going to present your drama to an audience, maybe to people outside your own class, you'll need to think about designing **posters** and **programmes**. Anyone with time to spare can do this.

You will need to spend some time with your group discussing progress. Everyone needs to know what is going on. **Time** needs to be allowed for actors to try on costumes and for sound and lighting cues to be worked out in rehearsals. You can use all the skills of negotiating and working with others which you have learned in presenting your improvised dramas.

Using different dramatic styles

There are many different styles in which drama can be presented. You will have seen this on television and in films as well as in the theatre. Here are **two contrasting styles** you might recognise:

★ **Realistic**

means as close as possible to real life. Actors move and speak in familiar ways; they seem like real people, interacting as we would expect them to do. For example, soap operas are presented in this way.

★ **Stylised**

means unrealistic, unlike real life. Actors move and speak according to the rules of a particular style: for example, melodrama (a sensational, exaggerated style of drama) very popular in Victorian times, with its Hero and Villain and a familiar storyline of love threatened by treachery.

Learning more from being in an audience

You can learn a lot about content, form and structure by seeing as many **different types** of presentations as you can: pantomimes, musicals, serious plays, comedies, opera, dance, children's shows, puppet shows, street theatre.

You will like some more than others, but you can learn from any live theatre experience. Don't underestimate the importance of presentations you see in school. It is helpful for Standard Grade pupils to have an audience; Higher students must have an audience for their presentations. Take any opportunities you can to see their work.

Whatever type of presentation you are watching, you should be aware of what the **content** is, and how it is being presented. What **forms** and **conventions** are being used? What is the **structure** of the presentation? How is tension built up? What are the **key moments**? Identify the **style** of the performance. What ideas could you use in your own work?

Building a Character

You need to find ways of really 'getting into' a character, convincing an audience that this is a **real person** and that what happens in the drama is important and believable.

Here are some areas to work on:

Age

It is important to be clear about **how old** your character is. In your group, you have to decide how old each character is **in relation** to the **others**. This has to make sense. A woman of 30 is unlikely to have a son aged 20! A man who is in his 90s could have memories of the First World War. Your character's age will help you decide on a believable history for that person.

Background

A real person has a **history**. Their background (what has happened to someone in their life before the events of the drama) makes them the person they are. Experiences in childhood, family life, at school, with friends, at work, successes and failures, problems with relationships – all of these affect the way someone is now.

Personality

Your personality is **the way you are** – you might be outgoing or shy, cheerful or moody. A happy, optimistic person will cope better with a crisis than someone who already feels defeated by life. None of us are the same all the time, but other people will often describe us as being a certain kind of person. Thinking about your character's personality will help you work out how he or she might behave in different situations.

Interests

Having ideas about someone's **interests** and **hobbies** can **help build your character**. These will be linked with the other decisions you are making about the person. A shy, middle-aged man might be keen on bird-watching; an energetic teenage girl could be a karate enthusiast. If you know what your character does in their spare time, you can bring that into the drama.

Name

Don't use your own name. Some people use their own name in role, but it does tend to hold them back from developing their character as a separate individual.

'Mum' and 'Dad' should really have names of their own – being parents is only one part of their identity.

Names should **fit the age** of your character: no-one over 30 is likely to be called Jason or Kylie; very few children are called Albert or Hilda today.

In a movement piece, your characters may not have names, but they could be 'Masked Figure One', 'The Leader', or 'The Victim'.

Giving your character a separate identity from yourself will help you make the part come alive for you and the audience.

Appearance

Some definite ideas about appearance will help you and the group to picture this person. What sort of clothes does he or she wear? Is he or she smart or scruffy; well-built or skinny? **Be sensible** about what each person can realistically achieve through make-up and costume. If you are small and lightly-built, playing a tall, broad-shouldered rugby player might not be a good idea! Boys playing female parts or girls playing male roles can sometimes be acceptable, but it is usually better to play someone of your own sex.

Language and voice

Getting the voice right can help you become your character easily in rehearsal and performance – it is worth working on. Language is **what** we say. Voice is **how** we say it.

★ **Register**

is a way of speaking **appropriate** to a situation. The way you talk to your friends is probably different from the way you would speak to the head teacher at school.

A teenager might use slang: 'No way, get lost!' Someone in authority, for example a doctor or bank manager, might use formal language: 'Good morning, Mrs Jones, what appears to be the problem?'

★ **Accent**

is a way of speaking which gives a clue to **where** a person comes **from**. It can also suggest social class. Putting on a 'posh' voice is a way of playing a well-off or snobbish person, but it can sound false. Use it with care. There is nothing wrong with speaking in your own, natural voice, whatever your accent is, if it suits the part. But if you want to sound, for instance, Welsh or Italian, one way of doing this is by listening to an accent and imitating the intonation.

★ **Intonation**

is the **modulation** of voice, rising and falling. For example, when you ask a question, your voice rises at the end: 'Are you coming out tonight, then?' A very firm answer would probably fall, signalling the end of the conversation: 'I told you already, no.' Chanting is a kind of intonation where everything is said on one or two notes. You can hear this at a football match: 'Ea….sy, ea….sy!'

★ **Articulation**

describes how clearly someone speaks. A television announcer might speak very precisely, clearly pronouncing every word; a drunk might speak very indistinctly, slurring his speech. The way most people speak is somewhere in between. You have to find a way of making your character sound believable with enough **clarity** to allow your audience to hear what you say.

★ **Tone**

is a **change** of voice to express emotions such as anger, sadness, hurt and pleasure. You could say 'I see you've had your hair cut,' in a way which would be taken as a compliment; said in a different tone of voice, it could be taken as an insult. **Emphasis**, stressing certain words, can change meaning.

★ **Pitch**

is the **variation** in height or depth of voice. Children and women tend to have higher-pitched voices than men. You will have heard the voice of someone who is upset or angry going higher as they lose control, or perhaps deepening with emotion. You can use this in acting, pitching your voice to suit the character and the situation.

★ **Volume**

is **loudness** of voice. In everyday speech, pitch and volume go together – we go higher as we get louder ('speaking up'). This is not always what you want when acting. Being heard even when whispering takes skill and practice.

★ **Pace**

is the **speed** of speech. Your character may be a cautious old man who speaks slowly and deliberately, or an impatient young woman who talks at great speed. Someone breaking bad news might speak slowly, with a **pause** between words; someone who has just won the lottery might speak very quickly, words tumbling out in excitement.

★ **Fluency**

is the way in which speech flows. A fluent speaker is smooth and confident.

It is important to look after your voice. Warm up; make sure you are prepared for a scream or shout without having to strain. Don't force your voice, use your breathing to help you project your voice – the audience has to be able to hear you.

Movement, body language and gestures

Movement, body language and gestures can tell the audience a great deal about a character.

★ **Movement and use of space**

You can pick up a lot about someone's mood by the way he or she walks and uses space. Someone striding down stage, head up, back straight, suggests confidence and purpose. The same person dragging their feet, moving into a corner, head down, shoulders slumped, looks tired and defeated.

★ **Body language and posture**

is something everyone recognises. You see it all the time, in school, for example: a teacher, hands on hips, chin thrust forward (aggressive body language, dominant posture) faces a pupil, arms folded, looking at the floor (protective body language, defeated posture).

★ **Gestures and facial expressions**

We can usually work out what different gestures (meaningful movements of the hand or arm) are intended to tell us. The raised fist, the finger to the lips or the beckoning finger all give clear signals. An angry or hurt look lets us know how someone feels.

Age and physical fitness can affect the way someone moves. An actor can play a young child by moving in a much quicker, less controlled way than an adult, or an old person by moving more slowly and stiffly.

Some people like to find the right shoes for their character – a farmer in wellington boots will walk very differently from a secretary in smart shoes.

Practise walking, standing, sitting down and getting up in role. Think about anything that might affect your character's movement – a tight skirt, a painful hip joint, carrying a heavy case. Giving your character a particular habit or mannerism can be useful – flicking hair back, nail-biting, standing with hands on hips, rocking backwards and forwards. First, however, you have to become aware of, and avoid, your own habits! Do you play with your hair, pull your sleeves down over your hands or always sit with your legs crossed?

Develop suitable actions for your character as you rehearse. Some business, such as combing your hair, unfolding and reading a newspaper, or chopping vegetables, gives you something to do and helps the audience believe in you.

Motivation

Motivation is the **reason** behind your character's behaviour. It is important in helping you understand how his or her mind works. Finding out about your character's motivation will help you know how to react, what to do and how to speak in different situations.

★ **Hot-seating**

One way to find out about a character's motivation is to spend some time in rehearsal hot-seating each character in turn. This can make a big difference to your portrayal of the character, because you have to think as that person, not as yourself. Questions can be asked about feelings, about events, about other characters, about hopes and fears and about the character's past and future.

★ **Writing in role**

is another way of getting into the mind of your character. This could be:

- a diary of the worst day in your life
- a letter to your mother in which you tell her how you feel
- your life story.

Relationships

Relationships with other people are **at the heart of drama**. Parents and children, friends and enemies, bosses and workers. Often people fight and argue – this conflict is what is interesting.

You need to know **why** your character behaves well with some people and badly with others. Working in role with others in your group, putting your characters into different situations, can help you find out more. For example, if you want to know why a man doesn't get on with his brother, you could take them back to childhood and role-play a scene where they play together, aged 7 and 5.

Think about **how** characters respond to one another. For example, a child enters during a scene where his mum and dad are arguing. Where does he move to? Why? What does the mum do? What about the dad? This is **interaction** (how characters react and respond to each other).

Status

Status is a character's **importance** – his or her position **relative to others**.

In some situations we look up to people because we see them as powerful, for example policemen, teachers and parents.

But they could behave in ways which might make us change our view. For example, a police inspector who took bribes and told lies would lose his high status. A boy who had low status because he wasn't good at Maths and English could gain high status by being the school's top goal scorer.

Status is not always connected with obvious power or control, however. Two people who appear to have equal status can gain or lose it because of events. This could happen in the course of a scene in a drama, through something which is said or done.

A useful way to work on status in your own drama is to give each character a status number from 1 to 10, with 1 being lowest and 10 highest. Is your character's status the same all the way through? The audience might see it as 2 when she is being told off by her mum about her untidy room, 6 when she's talking and having a laugh with her friends and 9 when she's asked out by the boy all the girls are keen on.

Learning more from being in an audience

You can learn a lot about building a character from watching actors in the theatre. Look at the programme to find out a bit about an actor's **background**. Sometimes there's a photo which can look quite different from the person on stage. Seeing the same actor playing different characters can show you how all the **techniques** you are learning to use can be put into practice. Notice how he or she moves and speaks. What gestures and mannerisms has he or she adopted? How is his or her **relationship** with other characters shown? Very often you see a character **changing** because of what is happening in the drama, making a kind of journey from ignorance to understanding. This can help with ideas for your own work.

Staging your Presentation

Once you have decided what your presentation is to be about and how you will perform it, you need to think about how to present it to an audience. Staging is the **formal setting** of a presentation. It involves working out where the audience will be as they watch the drama. In a theatre, there is usually fixed seating, with a raised stage, often at one end. In your drama studio or classroom, there will be a number of options. If you have rostra which can be used to build a platform, you can have a raised stage. You may have seating which can be raised. Raising the height of the audience or the acting area can make the drama easier to see.

Different types of staging

Depending on space and resources, here are some different types of staging to consider for your presentation:

★ **Proscenium stage**

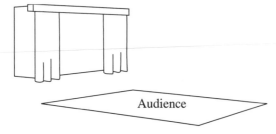

Traditional 'picture-frame' stage, raised, with front curtains; the audience seated in front of the performing area.

★ **Theatre in the round (also called arena)**

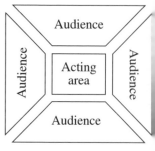

Audience seated on all sides, with acting space in the centre. This allows the audience to see the drama from different viewpoints; they are close to the action; actor's entrances and exits can be from all four corners. There will be times when some of the audience have a restricted view; this would have to be considered in rehearsal.

★ **Avenue (also called processional) theatre**

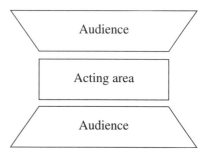

Audience seated on two sides, with acting space or stage down the centre. Fashion shows are often presented like this, with a catwalk for the models. This can be good for a drama with lots of action, where actors pass through the performing space close to the audience.

★ **Promenade theatre**

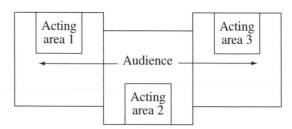

Audience stands and moves with the actors to follow the action, usually several scenes in different locations. This allows real audience involvement, especially in crowd scenes, but can be tiring for the spectators who will not always see everything.

★ **Thrust (also called apron) stage**

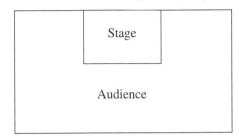

Audience seated on three sides. This has the advantages of theatre in the round, but with a 'back wall' which gives more room for a set and allows the audience a better view of the action.

★ **End stage**

Audience seated at one end; acting area at the other end. This gives all the audience the same view of the action, with more space in the acting area which can be used for scenery. It does distance the audience more, however, from what is going on.

To conclude, the best idea is to be **open-minded** about staging. It is very easy to get used to presenting your work in the same way every time. It can make watching a presentation much more interesting if you really think about how you want it to be seen.

Venue

A venue is **any place where a drama is presented**: a theatre, a classroom, a school hall are obvious places, but you could see a drama presentation in a park, a church, a street, a supermarket, a shopping mall, a car park… anywhere, in fact, that you could have space for performers and an audience. There is a theatre company in Scotland which presents drama in non-theatre spaces, even in people's living rooms!

Not all drama is suitable for every venue. A street performance would have to be eye-catching, easily understood and fairly short to capture the attention of passers-by. A church would be a good setting for a historical drama, with opportunities for using different levels. A school hall might need careful arrangement of seating to allow everyone to see, possibly using a floorcloth (a piece of heavy canvas) to define the acting area.

Learning more from being in an audience

Noticing how a presentation is staged can give you ideas for your own work. If you see the same play at two **different** venues, the atmosphere at each can be quite different. This can be because of the **relationship** between audience and actors. You might feel very involved, as if you are part of the action, in a small studio theatre with the audience on three sides. Watching a spectacular musical on a proscenium stage in a large theatre, you could feel swept along by what you see, but at more of a distance.

Target Audience

Deciding on the right audience for your presentation

You may have been thinking from the start of your work about who would be a suitable audience for your drama. By the time you are ready to present it, you will have a clearer idea. You might feel that your presentation is for a **general** audience – all ages, male and female, or that it would be appreciated more by a **specific** group of people.

Is it aimed at your own age group? Topics like bullying, divorce or drugs could be relevant to a teenage audience, especially if the main characters are young people. Perhaps your drama would appeal to a younger audience – a fantasy adventure or a puppet play. You might have chosen an issue which is relevant to all age groups – war, old age or the future.

How you put your ideas across will be influenced by your target audience. Using music from the current charts would appeal to a teenage audience; swearing would not be acceptable in a children's show. If your drama is going to be **effective**, it will have to be suitable for your audience.

Learning more from being in an audience

If you enjoyed a presentation, was this because it had things in it which appealed to you? If you were bored, was this because the play was aimed at an older audience, rather than because it was just not very good? Look at how other people in the audience **react**.

At a play like *The Steamie*, you will see many older women laughing as they recognise characters and stories from their own lives. Lots of younger people enjoy it just as much. Why?

At a pantomime or a children's show, the actors often get the audience to join in. What effect does this have?

Meaning and Message

Communicating what you want to get across to your audience

You began with an idea that you wanted to put across to others. The **meaning** of your drama could be very **simple**: two clowns juggling could just be for pure entertainment. But if you went on to show the sadness or pain in the real life of one of the clowns, the hidden feelings behind the painted smile, it would have a **deeper** meaning.

The audience should be able to make sense of the story, the relationships and the issues in your drama. Your aim is to make them believe in what is happening, to feel involved in what is happening to the characters and to think about the questions raised.

You may also have a **message** which you want to convey. The content of your presentation (what the characters say and do) will have conveyed some of your message. But you can add to this in other ways. A lot can be communicated **without words**. Here are some examples:

On a bare stage, a single empty chair is spotlit, waiting for someone who may never appear.

In a drama about a street accident, a child's shoe is handed to a woman who breaks down in tears. Each of these objects – the chair and the shoe – represents the person who is not there.

In a movement piece, a crown is taken from a figure lying on the ground and placed on the head of a seated figure. This shows clearly that the king or queen has been killed, and someone else is now taking their place. The crown represents power. These are all **symbols** which **communicate meaning**.

A set made up of hollow cubes is rearranged to form a barricade across the stage. A flag is raised and as the performers take their places with rifles in their hands, a cyclorama is flooded with red light. Sounds of distant gunfire. Images of war.

A single unmasked figure wearing white is surrounded by masked figures dressed in dark robes. Images of day and night, light and dark, good and evil.

Colour, lighting, set, props and sound can all be used to provide powerful **images**.

> When you are working on your ideas, be aware of how you can make use of symbols and images to help convey meaning.

You can put a message across by involving the audience with the characters, so that they share their experiences. This can be a powerful and effective way of making people question their attitudes and beliefs. For example, in a drama in which a child is knocked down by a driver affected by alcohol, the audience could be shown what led up to the accident and how the different characters would be affected by it. This would give a clear message about drinking and driving.

Key scenes, characters and events will help the audience understand your **purpose**. By highlighting important moments in a variety of ways you can make sure that your purpose is clear and your message communicated. You can heighten **tension** with conflict and confrontation. Or you could use **dramatic irony** where the audience knows something the characters are unaware of – for example, in a murder mystery, the audience know who the killer is.

It can be helpful to find out how your audience reacts to the presentation. Notice how closely they watch and listen to the action. What makes them laugh? What moments seem to hold their attention? Were they aware of symbols and images? Were they aware of a message? Ask them afterwards what they thought and felt about your presentation.

Learning more from being in an audience

When you are affected by what you see, try to work out what it is that brings a lump to your throat, what makes you laugh, what makes you angry. What was the meaning behind what happened? What mood and atmosphere was created? What was communicated through images and symbols? What message was being put across? What techniques were used to heighten tension?

Design

Design in the theatre means anything which the audience **sees** – the set (including scenery and furniture of all kinds), lighting, make-up, costumes and props. It can even include publicity materials like posters and programmes. The designer has to work closely with the director to make every aspect of the presentation look right.

There are many different ways in which a particular play can be presented. Shakespeare's plays have been enjoyed by theatre audiences for 400 years and presented in many different ways. Often it's the design that gives a familiar drama a different slant. You don't have to have the actors in Elizabethan costumes – they can wear clothes from the 1920s or the present day. This can help make the play more interesting for a modern audience.

The **style** of the presentation will influence the design. A realistic drama may need a set which looks like a real place, for example, a hospital waiting room or a library. A box set, made from flats which form continuous walls, with practicable doors and windows, could be used for this. Lighting would be used to give a **believable** indoor effect.

A presentation with a much freer approach to design might use painted backcloths and gauzes, moveable screens and rostra to create a number of different locations.

Lighting would be used creatively to add colour, to spotlight areas of the stage and for special effects. These would provide **mood** and **atmosphere** for the drama.

While you are working on your own presentations, you will probably not have much time to think about design as a separate activity. But you may have enjoyed experimenting with make-up and costume, and using colour in creating a set and lighting effects. When you are planning a drama and working out how to present it to an audience, think about how you want it to look.

Theatre Arts

Theatre Arts describes any practical additions which are made to enhance a presentation – **make-up**, **costume**, **sound**, **lighting**, **scenery**, **furniture**, **props** and **special effects**.

Technology is the hands-on equipment you need to get the effect you want – to make a sound tape or operate lighting.

What you are able to use depends very much on the resources available in your school. You might have a fully equipped drama studio with a computerised lighting board, sound system and dressing rooms, or you could be working in a classroom with a tape recorder and a box of props. What **is** important is that you know enough about Theatre Arts and technology to be able to say what you would use if you could.

You need to decide what effect you want and how you can achieve it.

Make-up

Do you need to use make-up? Make-up is used to allow **features to be seen** under bright stage lights and to help create a **believable** character or effect. What you can do will be limited by what you are able to use, but it is useful to think about what you'd like to do, if you had the time and resources.

It may be important for someone to look old or ill. This doesn't need to be complicated. You could get away with something quite **simple** – a pale base with some under-eye shading for the ill person, adding a bit more shading and some careful wrinkles to make them look old.

If you want to turn yourself into a threatening-looking criminal, you could darken your eyebrows, making them closer together, and give yourself some stubble using a dark cream shadow with a stipple sponge.

A powerful female boss might wear a strong red lipstick – that might be all that's needed. In a small performance space where you're close to the audience, heavy make-up is not necessary.

If you are presenting a futuristic drama, you may need very stylised, mask-like effects, using fantasy base colours like green or gold. Working out a design on paper first will make this easier to do quickly.

Perhaps a character is injured and has to be seen with a black eye or a wound. Bruises can be faked quite quickly with cream make-up in dark colours. Wounds and scars built up using soft putty or liquid latex will take longer. You might want to use a stage blood capsule in a fight scene for a realistic trickle of red from the corner of the mouth of the loser. This can be very effective but tricky to get right. It will need to be practised.

Do you have all the materials you need? Who else is using them? Where are you going to do the make-up? Work out designs, arrange to use suitable materials, do timed practice make-ups before your dress rehearsal. Allow time for applying and removing make-up. It's also essential to leave all the equipment clean and tidy.

Costume

What costumes are needed to make characters **believable**? Is the drama set in a particular **time** in history? You might need to look at some books to find out what people wore in 1700 or 1914. If it takes place in the future, you might use science fiction books, films or comics for ideas.

Think about **simple** ways of using costume to give the audience information about the characters. A white coat instantly suggests a doctor or a scientist, long skirts and shawls can help portray women from Victorian times, someone wearing a scruffy raincoat and an old scarf turns into a tramp.

Things that can be easily put on and taken off, preferably over school clothes, can save time and tempers.

Hats are very useful for quick changes of role, for example, policeman to builder. Personal props like briefcases and walking sticks can give the audience instant clues.

Can some of your group provide their own costumes? For a drama which happens in the present day you can wear ordinary clothes which could be borrowed from home. You want to find something which suits the age and personality of the character. Could you adapt something to make it look right?

Make lists with information about what each person needs and where they are getting their costumes. Arrange time and space for trying on costumes; find somewhere to store them until the performance.

Sound

What sound effects do you need? What music might you want to use before or during the presentation? Do you have percussion instruments like a tambour or tambourine, bells, chimes, or wood blocks that you can use?

You might use sound to **create a mood** – sad music from a film for an emotional farewell; birdsong at night for a secret meeting in the woods. A sound effect could **signal a key moment** in the drama – a doorbell announcing the arrival of the police; an air raid siren in wartime interrupting a family meal.

Will these be **live** or **recorded**? Sometimes it is easier to create a sound effect like a loud bang live off stage than to cue it perfectly on tape. You will need to find recorded sound effects or make your own. A suitable space and recording equipment will be needed as well as time to do this.

Your group will need to rehearse with the sound effects to get the timing right well before the presentation.

Who will operate the sound equipment? It has to be someone who has some knowledge of your drama and has had the chance to see it in rehearsal. A clear list of cues must be provided and time allowed for a technical rehearsal.

Lighting

What lighting effects do you need? What kind of **mood** and **atmosphere** do you want? Would it help to light different areas of the stage for different scenes, rather than having to move scenery or furniture? You may not have the resources to do exactly what you want, but it is worth thinking about what you would do if you could.

You might have a narrator sitting down stage left who will need to be spotlit when she speaks, with perhaps two main acting areas lit when scenes are presented in two different locations. This would need careful positioning and focusing of suitable spotlights. These would have to be patched (plugged into the dimmer board) so that the right lights could be brought up on cue using the control desk.

For a realistic drama about a family you might need a daylight or indoor lighting state. For a science fiction adventure you might want to create an unearthly, creepy lighting state. These could be achieved by using different colours, for example straw and pink for the realistic presentation; green and blue for the fantasy drama.

There are lots of effects you can create with lighting. For example, you could use a painted gauze to make someone appear and disappear: lit from the front it looks solid, but with a light behind it you can see through it. Gobos in profile spots can be used to project a range of patterns like leaves or flames.

What equipment can you use? What are the safety rules? Can you change the position and focus of lanterns? Can you use different colour filters (gels)? Can you re-patch if necessary? What needs do other groups have? Often it is necessary to negotiate and compromise if groups are presenting their dramas one after the other. A few general lighting states which will work for all groups need to be agreed.

Who will operate the lights? This has to be someone who has some knowledge of your drama and has had the chance to see it in rehearsal. As with sound, a clear list of cues must be provided and time allowed for a technical rehearsal. This is to make sure everything works the way you want it when you want it.

Scenery

What do you need to **create a believable set**? If the drama happens in several different locations, how will you manage to show these?

What rostra and flats are available? Do you have a free-standing screen which could be covered with paper or cloth to suggest part of a room? Is there a moveable rostrum (truck) which could be used in several different ways: for example, as a street stall or a boat? Can you adapt or paint these? Can they be put into place quickly and easily? Can you avoid scene changes?

Think about making use of cloth to create an effect quickly and easily – a rectangular wooden rostrum with cloth draped over it could represent a table, a coffin or an altar. A free-standing screen could be draped with lengths of material to show a curtained window, the entrance to a cave…

Furniture

What furniture is needed? **How** will it be positioned? Take time to place furniture carefully, especially chairs. Make sure you are not going to mask anyone by having chairs too close together. Putting furniture at an angle to the audience can be useful.

Don't have more furniture than you need. You will need room to move around it easily. You can suggest a hospital ward with one bed or a school classroom with a few desks. Small rostra and boxes can be used as stools and small tables. Mark positions of scenery and furniture with tape on the stage area to help with scene changes.

Props

Think about which props you need. These could be **personal** props which people bring on, carry in pockets or wear – a gun, a hankie or spectacles. **Set** props, which are used in the presentation, have to be in place on stage at the right time – a phone, a plate of biscuits or a book. Props can also be used for set dressing, to make the drama more **believable** – comics and toys in a child's bedroom, a filing cabinet and a pot plant in the manager's office. Can you make some props – a letter or a paper fan?

What will you need to find or borrow – a stone, a skull? Avoid getting carried away with having too many props. They can make your drama more complicated for performers and take time to set up and put away.

Accurate lists are very important. You will need somewhere to store things safely. You will need a props table off stage where all props are kept when not being used. Don't let people put anything else on this! Make sure props are returned at the end of each rehearsal and performance.

Special effects

For most of your drama work you're unlikely to be able to use much in the way of special effects, but it's useful to know what you could use if you had unlimited resources!

For a special presentation, you might be able to borrow or hire equipment. Even if you can't, you can write about what you would have done.

★ **A smoke machine**

   can provide atmosphere – a foggy Victorian street, a dream sequence.

★ **A strobe light**

   can turn a straightforward movement piece into a flickering silent movie.

★ **Pyrotechnics**

   Explosives, gunfire and flares can give a terrifyingly dramatic backdrop to a battle scene.

★ **Bubble machines and splurge guns**

   can be fun in children's shows and pantomimes.

★ **Traps**

   can provide dramatic impact, for example a figure rises up from under the stage, or a body is lowered into a grave.

★ **A revolving stage**

   allows you to have two sets, which can be alternated for transformations and other effects.

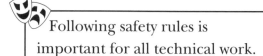 Following safety rules is important for all technical work.

Learning more from being in an audience

In the professional theatre, and in some amateur shows, you will have the chance to see Theatre Arts and technology used in **different ways**. Look at the effects and use your knowledge to work out how they are done. Shows like *Les Misérables, Grease* and *Joseph and the Amazing Technicolor Dreamcoat* use lots of special effects. If you are in a big theatre, look at the lighting rig – try to work out how effects are created. What colours are they using? Where are the lanterns positioned? Sometimes you will see something quite unexpected – for example, the stage centimetres deep in earth for Northern Stage's *Animal Farm.*

Preparing for the Exam

The exam, which lasts $1\frac{1}{2}$ hours, consists of two sections of compulsory questions: **Section A** is based on responses to the **Stimulus Paper** (which your teacher will give you to study several weeks before the exam); **Section B** is based on your knowledge and understanding of drama.

Working from the Stimulus Paper and preparing for Section A

★ **Make a good choice of one stimulus**

from the five in the Stimulus Paper. Your teacher will give you help with this. When you get the Stimulus Paper some weeks before the exam, take time to read and study it carefully. The five different stimuli in the Paper could be a poem, a drawing, an advertisement or any of the examples given on pages 4 – 7. Sometimes the stimulus that seems the most exciting to start with is the one you can't get very far with after a couple of periods. You need to be able to write well about this work in Section A of the exam, so make sure it has enough in it for you to use what you've learned. Remember that the stimulus is just the **starting point**. You can take your ideas in **any direction** as you create your drama. The more ideas you have, the better. You could try thinking of, say, two ideas for each stimulus, before you discuss the Stimulus Paper at all with your group.

★ **Get the best from group work**

All the skills you've been practising need to be used from the beginning. There is no time to waste. Reach a decision quickly on which stimulus to use. As far as possible, allow everyone to choose how to develop their ideas. Maybe you could each write a scenario at home. Take the best suggestions and try them out through role-play. Use your knowledge of form and structure to agree on a scenario which is workable and has a message to communicate. Keep your use of Theatre Arts simple, but have more ambitious ideas in mind that you can write about.

> Developing your characters fully, using all the techniques you've learned, is really important.

★ **Keep careful notes**

from the start. Your notes are the basis of your answers to Section A. There is quite a long time between doing this practical work and sitting the exam. There is no way you can remember what you did unless you write or tape it as you go along.

You must keep notes about:

- which stimulus you chose
- several reasons for your choice
- possible ways you could develop your chosen stimulus
- a scenario of your drama, showing which form(s) you are using, with a clear structure. Include time and place of each scene.
- details about your character – name, age, background, personality,

interests, appearance, voice, movement, body language, gestures, motivation, relationships and status

- ground plans for each scene, with a key, showing furniture, scenery, rostra and set props. Include position of entrances and exits. Show where the audience would be.
- ideas about your target audience, meaning and message, the kind of venue you would choose and reasons for your choice of form(s)
- details of Theatre Arts and technology, including ideas you may not actually be able to use: make-up, costume, sound, music, lighting, scenery, furniture and props.

You should now have what you need to prepare for Section A of the Examination Paper.

The examiner needs to know what you did in your group work based on the Stimulus Paper.

In Section A you must explain in detail how you developed a stimulus into a presentation.

You have to outline a situation suitable for acting out, showing that you know about form and structure.

You have to provide detailed, relevant information about a character; you must show that you are aware of that character's role and status in the drama.

You must describe in detail how your drama could be presented, showing that you have thought about target audience, staging and technical effects. You have to give reasons for these decisions.

The questions in Section A will cover the points in the box. They may not be in the same order each year. The wording may be different.

★ **Read the questions in Section A carefully and do what is asked**

The questions on character may concentrate on voice or movement or maybe on status. You may be asked to draw a ground plan for the first or last scene of your drama, or for any scene. You may be asked to think about a particular venue or way of staging. You may be asked to write about an important moment or scene and what theatre arts you might use.

If you have learned what is in your notes, you will be able to answer the questions in Section A.

Revising for Section B

You must not write in Section B about the work you did from the Stimulus Paper.
The way to revise for Section B is to use your work from the course. Everything you've done is relevant.

★ **You can use**:

- your presenting evaluations of yourself and others
- planning notes
- 'character cards' or other notes on characters you have worked on
- writing in role

- video and audio tapes of discussions, work in progress, presentations of your own work and that of others
- notes made during class work
- answers to practice exam questions
- designs – set, lighting, costume, make-up…
- reference books
- theatre programme
- reviews of productions
- discussion with your teacher and others
- questions from past exam papers.

★ **In Section B you could be asked about:**

- the drama process
- voice
- movement
- characterisation
- staging
- message and meaning
- relationships
- dealing with issues
- using research
- script work
- Theatre Arts and technology.

In Section B there are likely to be some questions which ask for essay-type answers worth up to 15 marks each. These could ask you about work covered in your course: for example, how you developed a character or what you learned by being responsible for technical work for a presentation. You might be asked to develop ideas for a drama either from a stimulus given in the question or for a particular target audience. To do well in these you will have to write in some detail. Remember that you can use sketches and diagrams to explain your ideas. There may be a question which tests your knowledge of theatre words. **Look carefully** at what is being asked for. Read **all** the questions before you start writing.

Sitting the exam

★ **On the day of the exam, you will probably be nervous. That's understood.**

If you've followed the advice about preparing for the exam, you will be ready and able to do your best. You have read through your notes the night before. You get up in plenty of time and arrive with a few minutes to spare. You have a spare pen, some tissues and your lucky mascot.

You are told to start. You have 1 hour 30 minutes.

The first thing you see is the Stimulus Paper. That's nice and familiar. It's the same one you saw weeks ago!

Once you've filled in all your details on the front of the booklet, put your pen down and look through all the questions in Section A. Read the questions **very carefully**. Notice **exactly** what is being asked for. Are you asked to do a Ground Plan for all or part of your drama? What information is needed about character – your own or someone else's? Use the marks as a guide to how much to write.

One possibility now is to get on with Section A right away. But have a look at the clock or your watch and work out how long you've got to do it. If you've spent 5 minutes reading so far, you've got 85 minutes left. You'll need 5 minutes to read the Section B questions, so that gives you 40 minutes to do Section A.

The other possibility is to do the Section B questions first. Which ones are worth 12 or 15 marks? Could you do them fairly easily? Again, look at the time. Leave yourself 40 minutes to go back to do Section A.

Whether you do Section A or Section B first, be strict with yourself. Don't spend 10 minutes on a two-mark question; don't use lots of extra paper for a six-mark answer – it's not worth it. If you're stuck on a question, leave it and move on to the next. Try to make a point or justified comment for each mark.

★ **Read each question carefully and notice how many marks it's worth**

Some questions may be divided into several sections. Make sure you answer them all. Look at how much space you've been given for each answer. You don't have to fill it all up – people have different sized handwriting – but it does give you an idea of how long your answer should be. If you have very big writing, you'll probably need extra paper.

> Don't panic! There's almost always a moment when you look up. You see everyone else writing madly. Your mind has gone blank. Use your drama training – take a deep breath, relax your shoulders, close your eyes for a moment and remind yourself that this is drama. You are writing about what you know.

If you have a few minutes left at the end, look back through your answer booklet and fill in any gaps in your answers. Don't be tempted to change things at this point. Your first idea was probably right. Make sure your name and question number are on any extra sheets.

Time's up! You've finished your Standard Grade Drama Exam. And you've done your best.

How is your work in Knowledge and Understanding marked?

Your final grade will be based on the mark you are given for the written exam you sit at the end of your course. This is marked by an external examiner.

The exam tests all the Knowledge and Understanding you have gained during the course.

> If you've worked hard and taken the advice given to you by your teacher and in this book, you will have got the most out of doing Standard Grade Drama. That gives you a good basis for going on to study Drama at a more advanced level. All the knowledge and experience you have will help you, whatever course you choose.

GLOSSARY

accent	way of speaking peculiar to an individual, locality or nation
acting	playing a part
action	events in a drama
actor	person playing a part
adopt	take on
arena theatre	acting area with audience on four sides
articulation	pronouncing words distinctly
atmosphere	feeling created by environment; scenery, sound or lighting
audience	people watching a presentation
avenue theatre	audience seated on two sides of performance space
backstage	non-acting area, often behind the stage
blocking	deciding where and when characters will move on stage
body language	mood or feelings created by physical positioning or movement
brainstorming	sharing and listing a large number of ideas
business	all actions on stage (e.g. opening a letter) except gestures
ceremony	religious or state ritual, formally performed
character	specific person in a drama
clarity	clearness
comic	humorous, funny
communicate	tell, put across
concept map	ideas represented as a diagram web
conflict	struggle, fight, argument
content	what is in the drama, subject matter
contribute	offer suggestions, help to bring about
convention	drama technique
convey	put across, communicate
costume	what actors wear for performance
create	make, bring into existence
cue	signal for speech, action or technical effect
cyclorama	large backcloth or wall (can be painted or lit) at rear of stage
dance	artistic expression through movement
deadline	date or time by which a task must be finished
develop	make more detailed, build on, expand
devise	create, invent
dialect	way of speaking peculiar to a particular local area
dialogue	conversation involving two or more characters
diction	verbal style, how someone speaks
directing	organising, taking responsibility for interpreting a drama
documentary	presentation of real life issues and events
down stage	acting area closest to audience
drama	representation of life created through acting
dramatic irony	situation where audience has prior information
effective	having an effect, achieving what was wanted
emotion	feeling
emphasis	stress
enhance	add to, improve

evaluate	assess, judge strengths and weaknesses	improvised drama	drama created 'on the spot'
expand	make bigger, develop	individual	one person
experiment	try out	initial	first, at the beginning
facial expression	look on face which shows feelings	inspiration	creative idea
filter	coloured transparency used for stage lighting	interaction	way in which characters behave towards one another
flashback	scene showing an earlier event	interview	meeting of persons face to face
flat(s)	rectangular piece(s) of scenery which can be joined together	intonation	modulation (rising and falling) of voice
floorcloth	canvas floorcovering (sometimes painted)	issue	point in question, matter for discussion
fluency	flow (of language)	justify	back up, prove with evidence
focus	central point, main idea	key moment	one of the most important parts of a drama
focus on	look closely at	lamp	bulb for stage light
form	how the drama is presented, overall style of presentation	language	means of communication, through spoken or written words
freeze frame	moment in a drama when action suddenly stops as if frozen	lantern	stage light
gel	alternative term for coloured filter used in stage lanterns	lighting grid	bar used to suspend stage lanterns
		location	place where the drama happens
gobo	thin metal plate cut out in a pattern, used in stage lanterns	make-up	worn on face to show character
gauze	thin fabric used for scenery	mannerism	habit of gesture or speech
gesture	meaningful movement of hand or arm	masking	hiding actor or stage area from audience
ground plan	bird's eye view of set, showing scenery, rostra and furniture	meaning	what is meant to be understood
		melodrama	sensational, exaggerated piece of drama
group	more than two people	message	what is meant to be communicated
grouping	how actors are positioned, relative to each other	mime	stylised form of movement; acting without words
hot-seating	questioning in role	monologue	scene in which only one character speaks
image	visual representation of an idea or feeling	mood	state of mind or feeling
improvise	act out without preparation	motivation	reason behind speech, movement or action

movement	all forms of physical expression through actions	**prop (property)**	object used by actor in drama
moves	actions performed by an actor	**proscenium stage**	stage within an enclosing arch
musical	drama which includes songs and music	**purpose**	intention
narration	telling a story	**pyrotechnics**	explosives, gunfire and flares
narrator	storyteller	**rake**	slope of stage (to allow actors to be seen)
off stage	area close to the stage, unseen by audience	**reaction**	response to what happens
on stage	in the scene being played	**realistic**	believable, like real life
pace	speed of speech, movement or storyline	**register**	way of speaking appropriate to situation
pair	two people	**rehearse**	practise, prepare for presentation
patching	plugging lanterns into a dimmer board	**rehearsed improvisation**	response to stimulus acted out after preparation
pause	break in speech or movement; short silence	**reject**	decide not to use, discard
physical	using the body	**relationship**	how one person or idea connects with another, how characters interact
pitch	variation in height or depth of voice	**relax**	wind down; get rid of tension in preparation for rehearsal or performance
portray	show		
portrayal	how character is shown by actor	**research**	find out information
positioning	placing of actors on stage	**resources**	anything which can be used
posture	how the body is held (e.g. upright)	**respond**	reply, react
		response	feeling, reaction
present	show to audience	**review**	look back on what has been achieved
presentation	drama acted out in front of at least one person	**role**	part played; attitude adopted
programme	information for audience which includes cast list	**role-play**	exploring attitudes and beliefs
project	(of voice) throw, make audible to audience	**rostrum (rostra)**	block(s) or platform(s) used to create a set at different levels
promenade theatre	audience follows action on foot, moving from one location to another	**scenario**	outline of drama
prompt	to give an actor a line he/she has forgotten	**scene**	part of drama set in one place and at one time
prompt copy	master copy of script in which all moves and technical effects are noted	**scenery**	backcloths, flats, rostra and other resources used to create place where drama happens
profile spot	spotlight which gives a precise beam	**script**	written dialogue for drama

select	choose	technology	equipment used to create effects such as lighting and sound
sequence	order of events	tension	excitement, build up of expectation
set (1)	scenery used to show where the drama takes place	theatre arts	practical additions to enhance a presentation (e.g. make-up, costume, lighting, sound, props, special effects)
set (2)	to position drama in a certain time or place		
situation	circumstances, specific point in drama		
slow motion	action performed at reduced speed	theatre in the round	audience on all sides
soap opera	television or radio serial concerned with everyday life	theme	subject, what a drama is about
		thrust stage	audience on three sides
soliloquy	speech in which actor speaks thoughts aloud	time	when a drama takes place (this could be time of day or historical period)
space	place in which drama is created or presented		
specific	definite	timing	speaking, moving, pausing or making effects happen at exactly the right moment
spontaneous improvisation	instant acting out of response to stimulus		
		tone	change of voice to express emotion
stage manager	person responsible for all technical aspects of presentation	topic	subject for discussion or for drama
staging	formal setting of presentation; way in which scenery is used	tragic	sad, distressing
		trap	trapdoor in stage floor
		truck	moveable rostrum, platform on wheels (for scenery)
status	position relative to others, importance		
stimulus	starting point, inspiration	up stage	acting area furthest from audience
storyline	account of events, main facts of drama		
		venue	place where a drama is presented
strike (a set)	clear acting area of furniture and props	voice	sound uttered from the mouth, created in the larynx
structure	way in which drama is presented, order of scenes		
style	way of presenting drama	voice over	words heard by audience spoken off stage or through sound system
stylised	using rules of a particular style, often not realistic		
		volume	loudness
tableau(x)	silent and motionless group of actors arranged to represent a scene	warm-up	exercise to prepare voice or body for acting
		web	concept map
target audience	specific group of people by whom a drama is intended to be watched		